CANADIAN DENTAL SCHOOL (CDA) INTERVIEW PREPARATION

Canadian Dental School (CDA) Interview Preparation

David King

Copyright © 2020 by David King

All rights reserved.

No part of this book may be reproduced in any form or by any electronic or mechanical means including information storage and retrieval systems, without permission in writing from the author. The only exception is by a reviewer, who may quote short excerpts in a review.

Printed in Canada

Table of Contents

Chapter 1: Introduction 1
Chapter 2: CDA Interview 2
    The Importance of the Interview 4
    CDA Interview Format 4
    Types of Questions for the CDA Interview 5
Chapter 3: Preparation for the Interview 9
    Brainstorming Worksheets 11
Chapter 4: The Interview Day 29
    What Happens on Interview Day? 29
    What to Do During the Interview? 29
    What to Do After the Interview? 31
Chapter 5: CDA Interview Experiences 33
Conclusion 38
Practice Questions 39
    Interview #1 43
    Interview #2 45
    Interview #3 47
    Interview #4 49
    Interview #5 51
    Interview #6 53
    Interview #7 55
    Interview #8 57
    Interview #9 59

Chapter 1: Introduction

The Canadian Dental Association interview for admission into a Canadian dental school is critical for candidates applying to the dentistry program. The stakes are high in these dentistry interviews as the future career and years of preparation are on the line. The competition is high with many highly qualified applicants. The interview is often the determining factor among the many competitive applications with high GPA and DAT scores. The candidates only have two attempts at the interview in their entire life at each school. A thorough preparation for the dentistry interview is crucial. Review the information provided as necessary. The information will prepare you for your interview. Learn an approach to manage CDA interview questions. Practice with practice questions to help you feel comfortable and confident for your interview.

Chapter 2: CDA Interview

The Canadian Dental Association interview for admission into a Canadian dental school is a standardized interview. The questions are created by the CDA and sent to all the schools. The schools receive the interview questions within a few days prior to the interview date. All the schools have the same set of interview questions across the country. The interviewers select questions from the interview question set. Therefore, a dentistry applicant can use the score performed at one dental school at another dental school application. The interview is structured the same every year. The interview duration is approximately 30 to 45 minutes. There will always be approximately seven questions. The questions are aimed at testing one or more of the competencies that have been outlined by CDA as qualities they desire in a dentist. These qualities are publicly stated. The qualities are generally expected in a health care professional. The interviewer is actively looking and evaluating these qualities in every question. The interviewee should aim to demonstrate that they possess these qualities when answering the questions. The applicant should recognize certain qualities the question is targeting, state the qualities they possess and support the statement with past experiences.

In general, the questions are designed to target mainly one competency per question. Once an applicant is aware of the qualities tested, it is usually obvious to an interviewee which competency is tested in each question. The applicant should have past experiences that demonstrate each of the competencies prepared before the interview. It is difficult to think of examples spontaneously during the interview, especially under the stress of the interview. Preparation facilitates the delivery of the experience in an organized and clear manner. The best way to prepare for the CDA interview is to start preparing early. Allow yourself time to brainstorm and recall past experiences that demonstrate the qualities desired by CDA. Use a chart that shows each of the qualities and complete the chart so that you have at least three experiences you can relay to the interviewer when the opportunity to demonstrate the competency arises. Once you've brainstormed the past experiences, you will need to practice organizing and delivering the past experiences as a coherent, clear, and organized story. You may want to write out the story of your past experiences and practice delivering the story in front of a video camera. Then evaluate the videotape of yourself searching for strength and weaknesses. Then work on the areas that you can improve. A useful structure for organizing your past experiences is known as the SAR structure. This structure is recommended for any situational type of question where you need to relay an experience to support your answer. The acronyms SAR represent Situation, Action, and Result. You begin by setting the stage of the story and briefly explain the situation. This will lead to your analysis of the situation and what you did in the situation. Finally, you end the story with a strong conclusion by stating the results of your action. Demonstrate that your actions resolved the problem outlined at the beginning of the story. Discuss any lessons you learned from the experience. It is important to have stories in which you've failed and learned something. It is common to encounter questions in which they will search or directly ask for situations in which you've failed at something. They want to know what you've gained or learned from the situation.

The Importance of the Interview

The interview is very important for entry into dentistry. All the applicants who are invited to an interview are selected and have submitted highly competitive applications. The main determining factor for admission into dentistry becomes the interview. Applicants can no longer rely on a strong GPA or DAT scores. The interview can be a decisive step in entering dentistry. The interviews introduce a "human" component to the often-impersonal application process. The interview is the first time the dental school can see and talk to the applicant in person. It is an opportunity to evaluate the applicant with more than the few pieces of paper in an application. The softer skills and people skills are vital in health care professions such as dentistry. The interview is an opportunity for the dental schools to evaluate social and soft skills of the applicant and is a critical component for dental school admission.

CDA Interview Format

The CDA interview is a structured and standardized interview. All the questions have been created by the CDA and sent to all the dental schools. The CDA interview is approximately 35 minutes in length. The applicant is interviewed by a panel of two to three interviewers that have undergone a CDA interview training workshop. The interviewers are general practitioners, faculty members, or dental students. It is important to note that the interviewers do not have access to the candidate's file. Hence, the score the interviewers assign to the applicant is solely based on the answers in response to the questions. The interviewers will ask seven questions. There are two versions of each question. The interviewers pick from a list of questions provided by the CDA. The dental schools receive the questions within a few days of the actual interview. The interviews are conducted at a dental school in Canada. Since all the questions and administration are standardized by the CDA, a CDA interview is equivalent regardless interview site. An applicant can use a score performed at a dental school for any other Canadian dental school. The applicant only needs to perform one interview and the score can be used for all dental schools in Canada. The applicant doesn't need to travel to another dental school for an interview. The interview score can be sent to another dental school, but you won't know the score of the interview. The applicant is only allowed two CDA interviews per school.

Types of Questions for the CDA Interview

There are two types of questions in CDA interviews. The types of questions are either situational questions or patterned behavior descriptions.

Situational questions ask the candidate what they would do in a hypothetical situation. An example of a situational question is:

> You are a babysitter for your supervisor's five-year-old daughter who is upset and angry about being away from her mother for the evening. She is hostile to you and frequently give tantrums. As you are cleaning up for dinner and give the daughter a glass of water, she splashes the water on your face and creates a mess. How would you react?

Patterned behavior descriptions are the type of questions in which the interviewer asks about a past behavior. The assumption for this type of question is that past experiences and behavior are good predictors of future behavior. An example of a patterned behavior description is:

Time management is an important as a dentist and as a student. Tell me about a time in the past that you had to deal with an important unscheduled situation that required your attention while having several prior commitments on your agenda. What did you do? What was the outcome?

One of the objectives of the CDA interview is to select applicants that are suitable as dentists. The CDA has constructed a list of qualities they believe are important for a dentist. As a result, the CDA evaluates the applicant on these qualities in the interview. There are seven qualities or "competencies" as referred to by the CDA. As a result there are seven questions, each question testing one of the seven competencies. Competencies are behaviors characterized by performance in realistic circumstances appropriate to your life experience. In other words, the CDA interview is assessing whether the applicant possesses personal characteristics that will enable the person to behave appropriately as a health professional.

The seven competencies are sensitivity to others, self control, tact and diplomacy, integrity, judgment and analysis, conscientiousness, and communication.

Sensitivity to others is being aware of and responsive to the feelings of others. As a dentist is a health care professional dealing with patients who are vulnerable, they need to exercise compassion and empathy to best help the patient. Patients commonly visit their dentist with apprehensions, fear, nervousness, and anxiety. Being empathic with the patient is important to putting the patient at ease and providing quality dental health care.

Self control is being in control or having restraint of oneself or one's actions, feelings, and thoughts. This competency is part of being a professional that provides specialized services based on the trust and confidence provided by the patient. A professional cannot be reckless. They must possess a certain level of self discipline to provide quality care and ensure the safety of the patient.

Tact and diplomacy go hand in hand. Tact is having a keen sense of what to say or do to avoid giving offence. It is possessing skill in dealing with difficult or delicate situations. Diplomacy is the skill in managing negotiations, handling people and etc. so that there is little or no ill will. These skills are important in maintaining positive clinician and patient relationship.

Integrity is the adherence to moral and ethical principles, having a soundness of moral character and being honest. The fiduciary relationship between a patient and the dentist demands a level of integrity for entrusting his or her health to the clinician.

Judgment and analysis follow one another where analysis is the process of studying the nature of something or of determining its essential features and their relations. Judgment is the ability to make a decision or form an opinion objectively, authoritatively, and wisely; especially in matters affecting action. A certain level of intelligence and analytical skill is required for the duties and responsibilities of a health care professional.

Conscientiousness is characterized by showing care, attention, and effort. A significant amount of work performed by a dentist requires a high level of attention and care. A certain level of conscientiousness is required to learn and to perform the tasks required of a dentist.

Communication is defined didactically as the imparting or interchange of thoughts, opinions, or information by speech, writing, or signs. This definition serves to remind the applicant that despite the interview being a verbal form of communication, the interviewers are also searching for other mediums of communication including written reports, presentations, and ideas outside of science and dentistry.

Chapter 3: Preparation for the Interview

The most important thing that you can do to help your interview performance is to prepare. The types of questions asked in a CDA interview will be difficult to answer on the spot. It is difficult to recall good examples one after another for several consecutive questions probing different competencies. You should be able to tie in real life examples for both the situational and pattern behavior type of questions. Hence, it is important to prepare for this type of interview by brainstorming past experiences related to the seven competencies. Once you have brainstormed past experiences for each of the seven competencies, you will have content that you can use to answer any of the seven questions they ask you. Sometimes, brainstorming can be difficult, especially when you are analyzing yourself. You should enlist family and friends to help brainstorm because they may notice or recall things you have long forgotten or shrugged off as unimportant but perfectly illustrate the competencies.

The brainstorming of past experiences to match the seven competencies should begin about three months before the interview. This will allow you time to brainstorm past experiences, sculpt and practice your responses, and give you time to improve and practice with mock interviews.

To help you with your brainstorming, the next few pages have been designed to organize your brainstorming. There is ample room to write your past experiences. Use another piece of paper if necessary. When brainstorming for past experiences for each competency, write any ideas that come to your mind and strive to fill the whole page. Spend at least five minutes writing nonstop filling in past experiences for each competency.

Brainstorming Worksheets

CDA Interview Preparation: Situation Brainstorming

Competency: Sensitivity to Others

Definition: Aware of and responsive to the feelings of others

Situation Examples:

Competency: Self Control

Definition: Control or restraint of oneself or one's actions, feelings, etc.

Situation Examples:

Competency: Tact and Diplomacy

Definition:
Tact: A keen sense of what to say or do to avoid giving offence; skill in dealing with difficult or delicate situations.

Diplomacy: Skill in managing negotiations, handling people, etc., so that there is little or no ill will

Situation Examples:

Competency: Integrity

Definition: Adherence to moral and ethical principles; soundness of moral character; honesty

Situation Examples:

Competency: Judgment and Analysis

Definition: Judgment: The ability to make a decision or form an opinion objectively, authoritatively, and wisely, especially in matters affecting action.

Analysis: The process of studying the nature of something or of determining its essential features and their relations

Situation Examples:

Competency: Conscientiousness

Definition: Characterized by showing care, attention, effort

Situation Examples:

Competency: Communication

Definition: The imparting or interchange of thoughts, opinions, or information by speech, writing, or signs

Situation Examples:

After you have finished brainstorming ideas, you will select three of the past experiences that you feel best illustrates the competency. The next step is to carve a well organized, concise, and compelling response with each of these past experiences. You need to create a story and paint a picture with your past experiences to illustrate the competencies. A useful organizational structure to construct your answers that still maintains the natural storytelling like effect is called SAR. The SAR is easy to remember and recall during the interview. The SAR structure stands for Situation, Action and Response. You begin your response by describing the situation you were dealing with and the dilemma or problem you were faced with. Then move onto to describe the action or the factors that you considered and the specific actions you took to resolve the problem or situation. Remember to focus on tasks that you performed and not to dilute your answer with actions done by other people. The interviewer is interested in you and your actions. After describing what you did to resolve the issue, this naturally leads to the result of your actions. The outcome of your actions could be positive, and you can triumphantly describe the benefits of your action. If the outcome was negative, you can describe the lessons you learned. Describe how it has made you more aware of yourself and efforts you've done to improve yourself. Not everyone is perfect. Having some past experiences that illustrate past failures and what you've learned from them will often become necessary in answering some of the interview questions. Some of the most difficult interview questions will ask for your weaknesses or worst experiences. Everyone has areas of improvement so you can't be honest and still escape these questions with blanket statements of perfectionisms. In preparing responses for weaknesses be sure to have clear lessons and efforts to overcome these challenges. But with some planning these traditionally difficult questions will become just another question that you have prepared to answer.

The next step in preparing for the interview is to practice interviewing by doing mock interviews. You can inquire with the career services department in your university or pre-dental interview help around campus for mock interview practice. You can also enlist a panel of family and friends and have them ask you interview questions. There are many interviews in this book that you can use to practice interviewing with different people. An equivalent to nine CDA interviews worth of practice and mock interviews are available near the end of the book. After you have practiced your mock interview, make sure you get feedback. Feedback is the most important method to find areas for improvement and to raise your interview performance. Have you friends and family comment on your performance or videotape yourself. Videotaping your interviews is very effective because you can review your interview many times. You'll often spot areas of improvement each time. You are often your hardest critic. Enlisting yourself by using a video camera is an invaluable tool. A tip with the video camera is to fast forward your video. Any mannerisms that you are oblivious to you normally will be exaggerated and become very obvious. You might notice mannerisms such as distracting gestures, fidgeting, awkward body language, and using filler words such "um," "like," or "ah."

Part of the interview preparation is planning out your outfit that you'll wear on interview day. As much as clothing is associated with fashion, the dentistry interview is not the time to make a fashion statement. Your physical appearance is the first impression that you will make. The health profession is still a conservative profession, so you want to dress accordingly. In general, a dark suit is recommended for men. Women have more options in terms of clothing and should still be conservative. In general skirts should not be above the knees, dress shoes should be closed toed and scented products used sparingly. Accessories should be modest so men should not elect distracting ties or tie clips. Proper hygiene is expected so men should groom their facial hair. Overall, the outfit should be aimed to look professional and avoid anything that would be distracting. One last note about the outfit is to practice wearing the outfit before the interview to avoid wardrobe malfunctions.

Chapter 4: The Interview Day

What Happens on Interview Day?

CDA interviews involve the applicant answering a set of standardized questions. The interviewee will generally sign in and convene in a waiting room where they will be called to an interview room. The interview rooms are usually small and cozy. There will be two or three interviewers composed of dentists, dental students, and faculty. The interviews generally last for about half an hour to an hour. At the end of the interview, the applicants are released either to go home or activities such as tours or presentations arranged by the school of dentistry.

What to Do During the Interview?

The first thing you should do the moment you enter the interview room is make eye contact. Acknowledge the interviewer by name and introduce yourself. Then shake hands with interviewers with a firm but not bone crushing handshake. Be sure to maintain eye contact and smile at appropriate times. Smiling is the easiest and most effective thing you can do to develop rapport with the interviewer. Unfortunately, many times the interviewee is too nervous and often forget to smile. Even worse is frowning or be stern faced during the interview. You want to look and feel natural and avoid looking stiff or tense. In addition, you want to maintain proper posture by not slouching. You also want to be mindful of negative body language such as crossing your arms, fidgeting, touching things on the table, and crossing your legs. When you speak you want to project clarity in your voice. Pay attention to maintain moderate speed and volume. Anxiety often makes people unconsciously speed up. The interview room is usually small so the volume of voice is generally not too loud otherwise a loud voice can overwhelm the room and be uncomfortable for the interviewers.

When presenting your responses, you want to be genuine and provide sincere answers. Acting or providing artificial answers are obvious and may be detrimental to your score and hamper rapport development with the interviewer. Try not to memorize answers to the point of providing stilted and unnatural answers. Injecting humor in your interview can help loosen the atmosphere and build rapport. However, only use humor if it comes naturally and if can remain professional. A useful tip is to pause and take a deep breath when needed to help you relax and not tense up.

After hearing the question, don't rush to answer the question even if you know what to say. You want to give a measured and deliberate pause before you answer to give you time to mentally prepare and to avoid appearing rushed. Take the few moments immediately after hearing the question to think over the question. In your mind, try to isolate the competency that the question reflects and use it as a guide for your answer. Before launching into an answer, always have a basic idea of what you want to say, otherwise you get bogged down and risk being circular in your response. A useful structure to organize your response is to structure your answer like an oral essay with a clear answer, supporting arguments, and conclusion. Your answer should aim to be clear, complete, thoughtful, logical, and sincere.

There may be a time when you don't know the answer to the question. Be rest assured that you are allowed time to think before answering. You can tell the interviewer that you need a moment to think of the answer. It is better to have a minute of silence than a minute of "umm…" So do not be worried that you are enveloped with silence while you think of a response. Be aware of the temptation to make up something up, especially for pattern behavior questions. If necessary, you can say what you would do if you cannot think of a past experience. If you continue to struggle with a particular question, you have a choice of moving to the next question and returning to the question later. This alternative will give you time to think of a response while you answer other questions. You might find inspiration for the skipped question while you're answering another question.

When you're answering the questions, the interviewers will try to guide you if they feel you are getting lost. Remember that for all of the questions, the why is more important than the what. You should always be honest because there are no right answers. You should always justify your response despite your belief. The interviewers are especially interested in your thought process and logic. In order to substantiate your response and make it more concrete, you want to incorporate a real-life example whenever appropriate.

What to Do After the Interview?

After the interview, shake hands, say thank you, and good bye, and leave the interview room. Do not dawdle after the interview but leave courteously. When you're done it is inevitable to self-analyze your performance and to reflect on the length of time of the interview. Some may worry that spending too little time was being too brief or spending too much time was being verbose. As you speak with other applicants you may become even more worried and confused as you get a mixture of stories. You shouldn't think too much about your performance as the only valid indicator of your performance is the feedback from the dental school and the admission result. Feel rest assured that most dental students don't know how well they did on their interview. The length of the interview may range from 25 minutes to 45 minutes, but the length of the interview is unrelated to the performance.

If you have any concerns about discriminatory behavior, inappropriate questions, or poor interview techniques, report to the admissions office before leaving. Remember, you are only graded on your answers to the seven CDA questions.

Chapter 5: CDA Interview Experiences

Stories from Applicants

Two short stories of interview experiences are presented from previous dental school applicants. The stories provide a first-person perspective of the interview experience. By hearing stories of prior interviews, applicants can get an idea of the interview experience and be better prepared for the interview.

Interview at the University of British Columbia

I had my interview in mid morning at 11 AM and walked up to the modern, gleaming Oral Health Centre made from glass and metal. An imposing structure resplendent with the latest architectural designs. I opened the glass door framed with metal and immediately encountered a smiling woman behind a small wooden desk ready to check me in for the interview. I gave her my name and verified against my driver's license and was instructed to go upstairs. Immediately behind the friendly lady was a spiral staircase. As I was walking up the stairs, I saw an applicant who just finished her interview. She left smiling and wished me well. I entered the second floor to witness a modernly furnished floor with hardwood floor. Immediately above me was a multicolored chandelier and in front of me was a large wooden reception desk. To the left of me was a lounge and eating area reminiscent of a premium coffeeshop. A lady met me at the second floor and escorted me to the side. I came early and there was one person sitting. We chatted and shared our mutual feelings of nervousness while waiting for the interview. Another jaunty fellow came out of his interview smiling and reassured us that the interviewers were nice, and we shouldn't worry. We waited on the armchairs and slowly the rest of the interviewees came, and we chatted, encouraged each other, and shared being nervous together despite the reassurance given by the people who just finished their interviews. As we waited a lady walks out from a hallway behind the reception desk. She calls out a name and one of the applicants leave with the lady. They both walked into the hallway and disappeared around a corner. The rest of the applicants cheered at the applicant who was called. Now the attention of the group of applicants was to look at the hallway in anticipation of the next applicant to be called upon. A few of the applicants needed to use the washroom, me included. After a few more minutes, another applicant was called in the same fashion and disappeared around the bend of the hallway with the remaining applicants cheering for him. The sporadically spaced times to wait punctuated by interviewers appearing and taking the applicant away continued. I waited and couldn't help but notice that almost all the applicants have been called in except for me a couple of other applicants. The anxiety mounts as the waiting continues near the end. We hear a pair of clacking sounds that suggests a pair of high heels coming from around the corner of the hallway. The clacking of the high heels becomes progressively louder until a bright, smiling young lady appears out of the hallway. She called my name and I leaped to my feet. I realized that being called has brought me relief in ending the anxiety building wait and sudden apprehension of the imminent beginning of the interview. I followed her down the hallway that I saw so many applicants disappeared before. To my surprise I was lead down a labyrinth of hallways that turned and crossed. I was thoroughly lost but simply followed the interviewer as she began some small talk. Finally, she stops in front of a door in the middle of a long hallway of doors. I didn't know what to expect when she opened the door. She let me into a small room and another interviewer was sitting behind a small desk. The interviewer got up to introduce himself and escorted me to a chair on the other side of the desk. The lady interviewer sat on the side of the desk while the male interviewer sat directly across from me. I noticed the age difference between the two interviewers; the lady was not much older than me while the male interviewer was in his 50's. I mentally guessed that the older interviewer was an established dentist while the younger interviewer was probably dental student. Shortly after the greetings they introduced themselves and confirmed my guess. The younger interviewer was about a year from finishing her dental program and the older interviewer was a dentist who also did some clinical teaching at the university. We talked and joked for a few more minutes before the interviewers pulled out their clipboards, explained the procedure of the CDA interview and began asking the CDA interview questions. The younger interviewer started asking an interview question by reading off the clipboard and jotted notes while I answered. Then the older interviewer would repeat the same routine. The two interviewers alternated in asking questions until all the CDA interview questions were answered. The interview ended with some more conversation. The younger interviewer again escorted me back to the waiting area.

Interview at the University of Alberta

It was beautiful sunny morning as I walked through the crisp morning air to the dentistry building at the University of Alberta. I walked into a stone building. I followed the signs that lead me down a hallway to a small lecture hall with cushioned seats where I signed in at the front of the lecture room. The seats were filled by men in black suits and women in business formal wear waiting for something. I sat and noticed that people were being called away by current dental students. After sitting and waiting for a while I was called by a young male dentistry student. He escorted me to the third floor of the building and took me to two large wooden doors that were slightly opened. My escort told me that the door in front of us was my interview room and waited for me to go in. All I saw was a gleam of light coming out of an ominously large pair of wooden doors that could easily have been an entrance to a large lecture hall. The thought of interviewing in a lecture hall was daunting and I hesitated to enter the room. But the escort was waiting and encouraged me to enter the room. I entered the room not knowing what to expect. The next thing that struck me was the small size of the room. The room was a small waiting area for a dental clinical room with a coffee table in the middle that was completely covered with neatly placed magazines and cushioned chairs around the coffee table. I was struck at the proximity of the three interviewers. A man in his fifties extended his hand to greet me followed by a young woman and a middle age woman. Through the introductions I learned that the man was a practicing dentist, the young woman was a dentistry student, and the middle age woman was an instructor at the dentistry school. The man explained the interview structure will be round robin. I sat down and I was facing the dental student with the man to the left and the middle age woman to the right. The middle age woman began the interview and read the question off her clipboard, followed by the dentistry student and then by the man. This was repeated a couple of times. The man offered an opportunity to add information at the end of the interview. The interview concluded with an exchange of handshakes and I was escorted out of the room where I saw my escort waiting in the hallway. The escort brought me down to the lecture hall where I waited with other interviewees. I noticed some interviewees coming into the room were anxiously waiting for their interview. After a brief period of waiting we were offered a tour of the school of dentistry lead by a dentistry and dental hygiene student. After the tour, the tour guides answered some questions, provided some information on the release of the admissions results and we were summarily dismissed just in time for lunch.

Summary

The interview building and rooms are not standardized. But the interview questions are standardized. Anxiety prior to the interview is normal. Standardized questions facilitate preparation. Preparation minimizes anxiety and maximizes performance.

Conclusion

The CDA interview is unique from typical job interviews. The preparations you've completed will equip you with valuable information. The preparations will prime you to provide insightful and organized responses for your interview. You will be ready for one of the most important interviews in your life. After completing the preparations, you can relax and complete your interview with ease and confidence. Good luck in your interview, admission, career and life.

Practice Questions

There are nine practice CDA interviews in this section. The questions simulate the CDA interview. Each question tests a certain quality. The questions provide an opportunity for you to recognize the quality tested. The practice questions allow you to practice answering questions and incorporating experiences that you've prepared. Answers vary and depend on your personal experiences. Use the approach outlined and incorporate your personal experience when possible. Video record your practice interview for self-assessment.

Practice CDA Style Interview Questions

Flip the page to begin.

Interview #1

1. Often, people find themselves in situations where someone is upset and gets emotional. Describe such a situation you encountered and how you responded.

2. You have a friend who is always late when you make plans together. You explain why it bothers you, and your friend promises it won't happen again. The following week, they are late again. How do you react?

3. You are attending a very important function where the dress code is "black tie". When you arrive to pick up your date, they are terribly underdressed. How do you approach the situation?

4. You are working on a group project and the deadline is fast approaching. Another group member proposes taking a shortcut to finishing the project by copying and pasting some information from the internet. Everyone else agrees, but you feel this is plagiarism and don't feel comfortable. How do you handle the situation?

5. People often encounter situations where they have to make a split-second decision. Describe one such experience and how you reacted.

6. You are a university student balancing a full course load and a part time job. You are also pursuing several hobbies and have an active social life. You are offered a very appealing but time-consuming volunteer position. How do you decide whether or not to accept?

7. Conflicts often arise in group settings. Describe a situation when you disagreed with a superior and had to explain your point of view.

Interview #2

1. Tell me about a time when you had to explain something to others who did not have any background knowledge about it.

2. You are the main speaker at a presentation which is very important to you. However, you are already over-loaded with work and maintaining GPA is also very important. What would you do?

3. Give me a time when you have provided advice to others.

4. Your friend tells you that she has questions for the upcoming test and she wants to share with you. What would you do?

5. Tell me about the time when you were treated unfairly from an authority.

6. Tell me about the time when you had to break a promise. What was the promise? Why was it important? And how did you deal with it?

7. You worked on your report for a week and you were confident about the report. However, the report was full of negative comments and the mark was not what you expected. What would you do?

Interview #3

1. If you were put in a situation where you were going overseas on exchange and had to leave tomorrow, but you just found out that your best friend's mother just passed away and was having a very hard time coping, what would you do?

2. Name a time when you were really angry with someone and how you dealt with the situation.

3. If you were a camp counselor and it was dinner time but the kids were really rowdy how would you try to settle them down?

4. If you got back an exam and you noticed that your mark was significantly higher than what it should have been (passing grade vs failing grade) would you tell the professor?

5. Name a time when you had to make an important decision and what steps you took to make your decision.

6. You are working with your best friend in construction, on a project and you notice that she is being very sloppy and careless. You know that if your supervisor came in and saw your friend being very careless with the project, he would fire him/her because he wants nothing but perfection. How would you handle the situation?

7. Name a time when you had to confront someone about something.

Interview #4

1. Describe a time when you felt very angry at someone/some situation. How did you deal with your emotions? What were your actions, and do you feel they were appropriate?

2. Imagine you were in a line to use the ATM machine when you notices a stranger standing in the same area and peeking as someone was entering their secret code. What would you do?

3. Have you ever gotten a mark that you think you didn't deserve (good/bad)? What did you do?

4. Canada is a very multicultural society, so tell us about a time where you had to communicate with someone who wasn't as fluent in English as you are.

5. Describe a situation when you had to share a secret that you promised a friend you wouldn't.

6. Imagine you were walking down a fairly empty street Downtown, and you noticed an elderly man shivering in the corner. You also notice some harmful material (needles/cigarettes) close by. Would you approach the man and offer him a meal/coffee? Why or why not?

7. Describe a time when you had a lot of work to do, and many social/personal problems. What did you do to resolve the situations that you faced? Would you act any way differently now?

Interview #5

1. When was a time you had to tell the truth to somebody even thought you know that it will hurt the person?

2. Your cousin wants something that you've cherished for a long time. What would you do?

3. When was the time you had to find the "middle-ground" in order to come to an agreement?

4. Tell me an occasion where you had to lie to an authority.

5. You see your friend shoplifting. What would you do?

6. You are late for very important interview, but you saw a grandmother fainted right beside you. What would you do?

7. Tell me one time where you had to organize an event that communication within organizers was critical.

Interview #6

1. What is integrity? Can you tell us a situation where you demonstrated this quality?

2. Assume you are a supervisor and one of you subordinate employees consistently arrives late to work. What action would you take?

3. Can you tell me about the last time that you had a conflict with a co-worker? How did you handle the situation? What was the outcome? In hindsight, what would you have done differently, if anything?

4. Describe the last time you had to make a tough decision. How did you handle it? How did things turn out?

5. A work colleague has told you in confidence that she suspects another colleague of stealing. What would your actions be?

6. You are giving a presentation where one member of the audience is continually stopping you and diverting you from the main part of the presentation. What would you do?

7. Think of a time when you've been part of a group, and someone said/did something that offended another within the same group. How would you react?

Interview #7

1. Tell us about a time when your first method of conveying an idea/instruction to somebody didn't work, and you came up with an alternative method of getting the message across.

2. You are working at a day camp and are paired 1-on-1 with a big 14 year old boy who has autism. He loves magazines and doesn't want to leave the magazine stand at the center. Your camp needs to leave to catch a bus, but the boy becomes upset when you try to get him to leave. He gets angry and punches you hard in the face. What do you do?

3. You've been placed in charge of running a kid-oriented community event, and have to supervise many teen volunteers. The majority of them are difficult to deal with, don't listen, do the opposite of what you ask them to do, and are basically acting like extra little kids. You've been receiving complaints from parents about his behavior, and it's only 11am. The event goes until 5pm. How do you handle the next 6 hours?

4. Your 16 year old brother asks if he can have his basketball team friends over on a night when your parents are out of town. You say yes, but basketball friends turn into 25 drunk and hormonal teenagers. What do you do?

5. Tell us of a time when you've gone "against the grain" and made a decision that was the right one, but not necessarily the popular one.

6. You've been put in charge of organizing a charity lunch for kids with various disabilities and special needs at a local hotel. How would you go about planning the event so that it goes smoothly?

7. Tell me a time when you had to tell bad news to someone.

Interview #8

1. Tell me a time when you completed a project and would like to do differently next time.

2. You are working at a grocery store and your supervisor tells you to pack the groceries in a way that would be slower. What would you do?

3. You are late in meeting up with your friends. Your younger brother asks you for help on his math homework. What would you do?

4. You are do poorly in your studies and broke up with your girlfriend and suffering a lot of stress. You want to take a year off from school. Your parents are angry at your decision and think that education is very expensive. What would you do?

5. There are times when you have a very heavy course load. Tell me how you handled a very heavy course load.

6. If you knew what you know now, what would you do differently?

7. If you were late to a meeting and half the group left and you're faced with the other half of the group and are staring angrily at you. What would you do?

Interview #9

1. How would you prepare for a presentation?

2. If you've taken all your courses and tried Dentistry twice and you didn't get in. What would you do?

3. Tell me a time when you had to deal with something complicated.

4. Tell me a situation when you had to face something that contradicted with your values, beliefs.

5. What would you do if your group didn't respond to you twice and you wanted to find out why?

6. What would you do if a person in the group constantly complains?

7. What would you do if someone in your group is performing slower than others?

www.ingramcontent.com/pod-product-compliance
Lightning Source LLC
Chambersburg PA
CBHW071415300426
44114CB00016B/2306